NEVER EAT YOUR CHICKENS

First edition.
ISBN: 978-1-7649283-0-4

For my daughter Yasmin and son Kai.

CHAPTER 1

THE EMPTY BASKET

Young Bob had spent his whole life in a simple but comfortable home. His mother cooked his meals, his father fixed anything that broke, and Bob had never gone to bed hungry.

But one morning, he decided it was time to leave.

Before he set off, his father handed him an old empty basket. Bob was not sure why he needed it, but he carried it anyway.

After several days on the road, his feet hurt, his stomach was empty and he was ready to stop walking.

Then he saw a small village surrounded by fields.

A wooden sign on the side of the road read:

WELCOME TO EGGSVILLE

Eggsville was unlike anywhere Bob had ever seen. Horses pulled carts along the quiet streets, chicken coops stood behind many of the houses, and almost everyone seemed to be carrying a basket.

Bob noticed something strange.

Eggs were everywhere.

Eggs filled shop windows and large baskets inside the stores. Outside the cafés, signs showed fried eggs, boiled eggs and omelettes.

Bob watched a baker hand over a loaf of bread and receive two eggs. A woman exchanged a few eggs for a hat.

He soon understood.

In Eggsville, eggs were both food and money. People ate them when they were hungry and used them to buy almost everything else.

Bob looked down at the old basket his father had given him. It no longer seemed quite so useless.

But it was still empty.

And Bob was still very hungry.

CHAPTER 2

THE FACTORY

Bob woke up early the next morning with his stomach rumbling. Everywhere he looked, people were eating breakfast—scrambled eggs, boiled eggs, omelettes...

A man in dusty work clothes walked past eating a large egg sandwich.

"Excuse me," Bob asked. "Where did you get your egg from?"

"I earned it," the man replied.

"You can earn eggs?" Bob asked.

The man looked surprised. "Of course."

"So where can I earn one?"

"They are always looking for workers at the basket factory," the man replied, pointing across the street.

Bob thanked him and hurried over.

The factory was impossible to miss. It was crowded and busy, with piles of straw stacked against the walls and half-finished baskets covering the worktables.

Inside, workers sorted piles of straw and wove them into the traditional egg baskets used all around Eggsville.

Bob stood near the entrance until a woman carrying a bundle of straw noticed him.

"I'm looking for work," Bob said.

The woman looked him over.

"Can you work hard?"

"I can."

She pointed towards a large pile of straw at the other end of the factory.

"You can start by carrying those bundles over to the worktables."

The work wasn't easy. He spent the day moving straw around the factory, stacking finished baskets and clearing the worktables for the basket makers. By the end of the day, his arms were tired and his hands were sore, but he had never felt so proud.

Before leaving, the workers were each paid one egg for their work.

When Bob's turn came, the factory manager placed one egg into his empty basket.

"You earned it," he said.

Bob looked down at the egg.

The first egg he had ever earned.

That evening, he ate it for dinner. It wasn't a feast, but it was enough.

The next morning, Bob woke with an empty basket and happily went back to work.

CHAPTER 3

THE MAN WHO ALWAYS STARTS AGAIN

Bob settled into his new job at the basket factory. Every morning he arrived early, worked hard throughout the day and earned one egg before heading home. He liked the job, the people were friendly and he was proud to be earning his own eggs.

He often found himself chatting with one of the older workers.

One afternoon, Bob asked, "How long have you been working here?"

The older worker thought for a moment.

"Oh... about thirty years."

"Thirty years?"

Bob looked down at the worker's basket. Just like his own, it was empty.

"Do you always start the day with an empty basket?"

"Every morning," the worker replied without hesitation.

That evening, they both earned their usual egg before heading home.

The next morning, Bob saw the older worker arrive with an empty basket once again.

"So... you start again every day?" he asked.

"Yep. Every single day."

The older worker was kind. He worked hard. He had been working at the factory for thirty years. Yet every morning, he started again with an empty basket.

Some people earn an egg every day and eat it every night.

CHAPTER 4

THE BASKET SHOP

One afternoon, as Bob walked home from the basket factory, a beautiful shop caught his attention.

It was the finest shop he had seen in Eggsville. Behind the large display window were baskets of every shape and size.

Bob stopped for a closer look.

Several customers came and went, each carrying a new basket. Some chose small baskets for carrying only a few eggs. Others bought strong baskets suitable for farm work. A few chose lighter baskets for carrying around town.

Every basket seemed to have a purpose, and every customer seemed to find exactly the one they needed.

The basket factory made excellent baskets, but this place felt different. It was quiet, clean and welcoming.

"I'd like to work here one day," Bob thought.

A few days later, he gathered the courage to walk inside.

Behind the counter stood a well-dressed man with a neat moustache.

"How can I help you?"

"I'm looking for a job," Bob replied.

The shop owner studied him for a moment.

"Have you ever worked in a shop before?"

"No. But I work at the basket factory."

"Good. Then you already know something about baskets."

"So... can I work here?"

The shop owner thought about it.

"I think you can. But you'll be starting in the back room."

"Everyone starts there," the owner explained. "Before you can help people choose baskets, you must first know every kind of basket in this shop."

Bob didn't need much convincing.

"I'll be here first thing tomorrow morning."

The next morning, Bob arrived early.

The back room was packed with baskets from floor to ceiling. More arrived throughout the day. Bob unpacked them, stacked them neatly and carried them to the front whenever the displays needed refilling.

It wasn't the job he had imagined.

But he liked the shop, and he was happy to be there.

Before he left that evening, the shop owner handed him one egg.

"Thank you for your hard work today."

Bob thanked him and headed home.

It was still only one egg.

But somehow, it didn't matter.

Bob knew he had made the right choice.

A better place doesn't always mean more eggs.

CHAPTER 5

EVENING LESSONS

Bob enjoyed working at the basket shop.

During the day he unpacked baskets, stacked them neatly and kept the displays full. Whenever he had a spare moment, he watched the people working at the front of the shop.

Their knowledge amazed him. They could tell where a basket had been woven, what kind of straw had been used and how many years it would last just by looking at it. They knew what each basket was worth, which one was easier to carry, which could hold the heaviest load and which was best for each job.

One evening, just before going home, Bob approached the shop owner.

"One day, I'd like to help customers choose baskets."

"It looks easy," said the shop owner, "but there is much more to it. To help people choose the right basket, you must understand every kind of basket, what it can do and why someone would choose it."

"How do I learn all that?" Bob asked.

"It takes years," the owner replied. "The people working at the front have studied baskets for a long time."

"Can I learn too?"

"Of course. The Eggsville School of Baskets holds lessons every evening."

From the following week, Bob worked at the shop during the day and studied baskets at night. He learned about different kinds of straw and other materials used to weave them. He studied how size, weight and quality could change the way a basket felt, what it could carry and how many eggs it was worth.

He learned about the legendary basket designers of Eggsville—the ones who created baskets that stayed dry in the rain, folded into tiny spaces or looked nothing like any basket before them. He even saw rare baskets from distant parts of Eggsville, each with its own unusual style.

Bob continued working in the back room and studying after work. He still earned one egg each day and ate it for dinner, just as he always had.

CHAPTER 6

THE EXTRA EGG

One morning, someone who worked at the front of the shop was away.

The shop owner called Bob over.

"You'll be helping customers today."

Bob wasn't expecting that.

"Me?"

"Sure. You've been studying baskets every evening. I think you're ready."

Bob took a deep breath and walked to the front of the shop.

A man soon walked in carrying a worn-out basket. It had a large hole in one side and a couple of old banana peels inside. Judging by the smell, they had been there for a while.

"Good morning," Bob said. "How can I help you today?"

"Morning. I'm looking for a new basket."

"I grow bananas, you see," the man added. "Every Saturday I carry them to the Eggsville Market. This one's been serving me well for years, but..."

He looked down at the large hole.

"It's seen better days."

"I think it might be time for a new one," Bob said.

He picked up a basket from the shelf.

"I think this one would suit you well. It's woven from stronger straw, the large handles are more comfortable to carry, and the wider base will help stop your bananas from getting squashed on the walk to the market."

The man turned the basket over in his hands.

"How many eggs does it cost?"

"Five eggs."

"Ouch..."

The man frowned.

"I'm afraid I only have two."

Bob quickly found another basket.

"This one is slightly smaller and made from ordinary straw. It might not last quite as long, but it's still strong enough for carrying bananas. And it costs only two eggs."

"I'll take it!"

As the day went on, more people came through the door. Some already knew what they wanted. Others needed Bob's help.

By the time the shop closed, he had helped more people than he could remember.

As everyone was getting ready to leave, the shop owner handed him two eggs.

“You sold ten baskets today. Around here, that's worth an extra egg.”

That evening, Bob cooked one egg for dinner, just as he always did.

He looked at the second egg.

He wasn't hungry anymore.

So he placed it carefully back into his basket.

CHAPTER 7

MORE EGGS

Some days the shop was quiet. Other days, people kept walking through the door.

Bob continued working in the back room and selling baskets at the front whenever he was needed.

On the busier days, he even earned an extra egg.

He still ate one egg for dinner, just as he always had, and kept the extra one in his basket.

Nothing else really changed.

Slowly but surely, the eggs began to add up in Bob's old basket.

He never counted them.

He simply left them there.

CHAPTER 8

THE LITTLE GIRL

Not everyone who walked into the basket shop left carrying a new basket.

Parents often came in with their children. Sometimes they couldn't find the right basket. Sometimes they were hoping to spend fewer eggs. And sometimes their children simply wouldn't let them shop in peace.

Most children had very little interest in baskets. Bob couldn't blame them.

While their parents looked around the shop, they wandered between the shelves looking bored.

Every few minutes, an impatient child would ask,

"Mum... can we go now?"

Others were far more energetic. They picked up baskets, carried them around the shop and rarely put them back where they belonged.

The shop owner wasn't particularly fond of children running around his shop.

Bob didn't mind.

He liked talking to them. They made his day more interesting.

One morning, a lady came in holding the hand of a little girl wearing a bright pink dress. The girl stayed close to her mother as they looked around the shop.

After a few minutes, they turned towards the door.

"Excuse me," Bob said. "Did you find what you were looking for?"

"No, I'm afraid we didn't."

"We have some baskets made especially for children," Bob said. "They're at the back of the shop."

"Ahh yes, I've seen them, but she didn't like any of them."

The little girl suddenly held up her doll.

"It's for Dolly!" she announced loudly.

"I want a basket to carry her."

Bob looked at the doll.

She was wearing a little pink dress...

Just like the little girl.

The lady thanked him, took her daughter's hand and headed for the door.

For the rest of the afternoon, Bob couldn't stop thinking about what the little girl had said.

He looked around the shop. There were baskets of every size. Some were deeper. Some were wider. Some had different handles or patterns woven into the straw. But somehow, they still all looked the same.

They were all brown.

They were all made from straw.

Most were designed for work.

Even the children's baskets looked just like the others.

Only smaller.

CHAPTER 9

BAD IDEAS

That evening, Bob sat down with a pencil and a piece of paper.

He wanted to make the little girl a basket she would love.

He began sketching one idea after another.

The first was tiny. It looked more like a basket for the doll than for the little girl.

The second was square.

He stared at it... Nope.

The third looked beautiful, but it was far too complicated to weave and would cost too many eggs.

Bob gave up on sketching and decided to try building one instead.

He made a little basket with a perfectly round base. But the moment he set it down, it rolled across the floor.

The next one was so light that it bent as soon as he placed the first egg inside.

After many more attempts, Bob finally built a basket he really liked.

Excited to show the shop owner, he took it to work and proudly set it on the counter.

The shop owner examined it carefully from every angle before finally saying,

"It's certainly different."

Bob waited.

"But where do the eggs go?"

Bob stared at his creation.

"Oh, come on... for egg's sake!" he muttered.

He had forgotten to leave an opening.

That night, he went back to sketching.

Night after night, he kept sketching, building and trying new ideas.

But none of them felt right.

CHAPTER 10

BOB'S BASKETS

Bob remembered the little girl and her doll.

"Little girls certainly seem to like pink," he thought.

That evening, he tried something different. He took some ordinary straw, carefully coloured it and began weaving a small basket. When he finished, it looked nothing like the baskets at the shop.

It was pink.

Bob made another. Then another.

By the weekend, he had enough to take and sell at the Eggsville Market, the busiest place in town. He found a great little spot between the food stalls and set up his pink basket stand. He even made a small handwritten sign:

BOB'S BASKETS

The market was packed that day, but hardly anyone paid attention to Bob's baskets.

Then a young girl spotted them.

"Mum, look at those!"

She hurried over, pulling her mother along with her.

Soon, more children were pulling their parents towards Bob's stand.

By the end of the day, he had sold several pink baskets and earned a few extra eggs. He continued working at the basket shop and began selling his pink baskets at the Eggsville Market on weekends.

Every evening, he ate one egg for dinner and added any extra eggs straight into his basket.

CHAPTER 11

eBASKET

At the Eggsville Market, there was a tall man with round glasses and a carefully groomed beard. Everyone seemed to know who he was. He dressed simply and spoke quietly, but people said he was one of the richest men in Eggsville. Some even said his farm was worth millions of eggs.

One Saturday, Bob noticed a large crowd gathered around him. The man was holding something he had never seen before.

“This,” he announced, “is the eBasket.”

The eBasket looked nothing like an ordinary basket. It was small and perfectly rounded, with no sharp edges and no handles. It was about half the size of a normal straw basket and looked like it could carry only three eggs.

But it was beautiful.

Instead of straw, it was made from a smooth, polished material that seemed to shine in the sun.

The man held it up for everyone to see.

“The eBasket isn't just a new basket,” he claimed. “It's the future of carrying eggs.”

He turned it slowly in his hand.

“Smaller. Lighter. Better.”

He slipped three eggs inside the eBasket.

“Three eggs have never travelled in such style.”

People in the crowd whispered to each other as they tried to get a closer look. By the end of the presentation, everyone seemed to be talking about the new eBasket. Even Bob had to admit, it was pretty impressive.

It wasn't long before eBaskets started appearing all around Eggsville. They were especially popular among younger people like Bob. Soon, everyone wanted to be seen carrying one. eBaskets were made in another town, and only a small number arrived in Eggsville each week, carried by donkey directly to the Eggsville Market.

An eBasket wasn't cheap. It cost one hundred eggs.

CHAPTER 12

ONE HUNDRED EGGS

Life stayed pretty simple for Bob.

He worked at the basket shop, made pink baskets in his spare time and sold them at the Eggsville Market on weekends.

Some days he earned an extra egg or two. Other days he didn't.

Whenever there were eggs left over, he added them to the old basket his father had given him.

One evening, after eating his usual egg for dinner, Bob picked up the basket.

It was getting heavy.

"I wonder how many eggs I've got," he thought.

He emptied them onto the table and started counting.

Ten.

Twenty.

Fifty.

He kept going.

Ninety-eight.

Ninety-nine.

One hundred.

"Wow," Bob said out loud.

He had never had so many eggs in his life.

CHAPTER 13

HEALTHY CHICKENS

Bob arrived at the Eggsville Market carrying one hundred eggs in his old basket.

He knew exactly what he wanted.

The new eBasket 5 had just arrived.

It was even lighter than the original eBasket, could carry two extra eggs and now came with a small side pocket for keeping your favourite egg recipes.

For five extra eggs, you could even have your name engraved on the back.

Bob picked one up.

It felt incredible.

Then he looked down at his old basket.

The straw was faded. The handle was worn and several strands of straw were sticking out from the sides.

It was the same basket his father had given him when he first left home. He had carried his first earned egg in it. But now... it looked pretty old.

"I've worked hard," he thought. "I deserve a new basket."

The eBasket cost one hundred eggs. Exactly what he had saved.

Bob stood there considering it.

"Chickens! Healthy chickens!"

A loud voice called from behind him.

"One hundred eggs each!"

Bob turned around.

A few steps away from the beautiful eBasket display was an old wooden chicken stand. A woman stood behind a low wooden fence with several lively chickens wandering around behind her.

"Healthy chickens! One hundred eggs each!" she called again.

The chickens wandered around noisily.

Bob looked at them.

"Do they lay eggs?" he asked.

"Every morning," the woman said. "Fresh ones."

Bob glanced back at the polished eBasket 5.

Then at the chickens.

He could spend his one hundred eggs on the shiny new eBasket...

or he could buy a chicken.

CHAPTER 14

HENRY

"You look confused."

An old man was standing right next to him. He had a weathered face and enormous grey eyebrows.

"A little," Bob admitted.

The old man looked closely at the eBasket in Bob's hand.

"Nice basket."

"It is," Bob said.

Then he looked at the chicken.

"Nice chicken too," he mumbled, almost as if he was the one who had to make the decision.

Bob laughed.

"It's just a chicken."

"Ahh," said the old man. "So what's the problem?"

"I've been saving for a long time. I finally have one hundred eggs, and this is the new eBasket 5."

"And?" asked the old man.

"I want it."

"Then buy it."

Bob wasn't expecting that.

The old man started to walk away.

“Wait,” Bob said. “What about the chicken?”

The old man turned around.

“What about it?”

“It costs the same as the eBasket.”

“Does it?” the old man asked.

“Yes,” Bob said confidently. “One chicken. One hundred eggs.”

“And what about tomorrow?”

Bob wasn't sure what he meant.

“Tomorrow?”

The old man pointed at the chicken.

Bob thought for a moment.

“Ahh... the chicken would lay a fresh egg every day.”

“And the basket?”

Bob looked down at the shiny eBasket in his hand.

“Nothing, I guess.”

The old man gave a small shrug.

“Interesting,” he said quietly and began walking away again.

“Wait!” Bob called. “What's your name?”

“Henry.”

Bob watched the strange old man disappear into the busy market.

A little disappointed, he carefully placed the eBasket back in its display.

“I'll take one,” Bob said to the chicken seller as he handed her his hard-earned one hundred eggs.

Bob left the market with his old basket.

No eggs.

No eBasket.

And one very noisy chicken.

But the next morning, he found a fresh egg waiting for him.

CHAPTER 15

THE SECOND CHICKEN

Every morning, Bob's chicken laid a fresh egg.

He would find it waiting for him, pick it up and place it in his old basket.

The next morning, there was another egg.

And the morning after that, another.

"The woman was right," he thought. "This really is a healthy chicken."

The eggs in his basket began to add up again.

Eventually, Bob had saved enough to buy another chicken.

He picked up his basket and headed back to the Eggsville Market.

The chicken seller was still there, with several healthy-looking chickens for sale. A wooden sign hanging above her stand read:

HEALTHY CHICKENS
100 EGGS EACH

"I'll take one."

He handed over one hundred eggs and headed home with his second chicken.

The next morning, Bob found two fresh eggs waiting for him. One from each chicken.

And now, every morning, Bob would get two eggs instead of one.

CHAPTER 16

MORE CHICKENS

With two healthy chickens, Bob now found two fresh eggs waiting for him every morning. His basket began filling twice as fast.

When he had saved enough, he bought his third chicken.

Three chickens meant three fresh eggs every morning.

Bob kept saving his eggs, and soon three chickens became four.

His old basket was filling faster than ever.

One day, when he had enough eggs for another chicken, he returned to the Eggsville Market.

As he approached the chicken stand, he spotted Henry nearby, quietly observing the noisy chickens.

Henry recognised Bob and noticed his basket full of eggs.

"Already buying another chicken?"

"Yep."

"How many do you have now?"

"Four."

Henry looked at Bob's basket.

"So why do you need another one?"

For a moment, Bob wasn't quite sure how to answer.

Then he thought about his chickens.

"My four chickens give me four fresh eggs every morning. If I buy another chicken, I'll get five."

"And my basket will fill even faster," Bob added.

"So what will you do when it fills again?"

Bob knew the answer this time.

"Buy another chicken."

Henry gave him an approving look, then slowly walked away.

The more chickens he had, the more eggs he received every morning.

And the more eggs he received, the sooner he could buy another chicken.

Bob handed the chicken seller one hundred eggs and headed home with his fifth healthy chicken.

The next morning, five fresh eggs were waiting for him.

More chickens bring more eggs. More eggs bring more chickens.

CHAPTER 17

THE BARGAIN CHICKEN

One day, Bob returned to the Eggsville Market with enough eggs to buy another healthy chicken.

But before he reached the usual chicken stand, a large sign caught his attention.

BARGAIN CHICKENS
ONLY 50 EGGS!

"Half the price!" shouted the seller. "Best bargain in Eggsville!"

Bob was tempted.

Fifty eggs was much cheaper than one hundred.

He looked at one of the bargain chickens. Her feathers were untidy and she looked a little tired.

"Does she lay eggs?" Bob asked.

"Of course!" said the seller.

"Every morning?"

The seller hesitated.

"Well... some mornings."

Bob looked at the scruffy chicken again.

"How often?"

The seller suddenly became very interested in rearranging a pile of straw beside his stand.

Bob picked up his basket and continued towards the healthy chicken stand.

A cheap chicken is not a bargain if you cannot count on her eggs.

CHAPTER 18

THE GREAT ROOSTER SHOW

Music and cheering echoed across the Eggsville Market.

A large crowd had gathered around a colourful new stand.

"Come and see the greatest young roosters in Eggsville!" called the seller. "Buy one today and it could be worth twice as many eggs next year!"

Bob made his way through the crowd.

One rooster immediately caught his attention. He was young and strong, with bright feathers and a magnificent red tail.

"How many eggs does he lay?" Bob asked.

The seller laughed.

"None. He's a rooster."

"Then how will he give me more eggs?"

"He won't," said the seller. "But he's still young. As he grows bigger and stronger, he could become much more valuable. Then you can sell him."

"So someone will pay me more eggs for him later?"

"Probably."

"There are no guarantees," added the seller.

Bob looked at the rooster again. His chickens gave him fresh eggs every morning. The young rooster would give him nothing today but might be worth far more someday.

Just as he was considering whether to buy him or not, old Henry appeared through the crowd.

“Thinking about getting a rooster this time?”

“Maybe,” Bob said.

Henry glanced at the colourful bird.

“There is nothing wrong with owning a rooster.”

“Just don't expect breakfast from him.”

CHAPTER 19

THE MAN WHO ATE EVERYTHING

Bob once met a man who owned ten healthy chickens.

Every day, his chickens laid ten fresh eggs.

"Ten eggs a day!" Bob said. "Your basket must be full."

The man shook his head.

"For breakfast, I eat three fried eggs. For lunch, I have a four-egg omelette. And for dinner, I have a three-egg pie."

"So how many eggs do you save?" Bob asked.

"None," said the man. "But I have ten chickens!"

The next day, his chickens laid ten more eggs.

The man ate every one of them.

His chickens kept producing, but his basket stayed empty.

It does not matter how many eggs you receive if you eat all of them.

CHAPTER 20

DOCTOR JESS

Bob woke up with his stomach feeling a little strange.

By lunchtime, it still didn't feel right, so he went to see Doctor Jess. Her clinic was small and tidy. Hanging on the wall behind her desk was a framed certificate:

DR JESSICA PARKER

EGGSVILLE SCHOOL OF MEDICINE

Doctor Jess examined Bob's stomach.

"Have you eaten anything unusual?"

"Not really," Bob said. "I had my usual egg for dinner last night."

"Although... that egg did look a little off."

"That could explain it," said Doctor Jess. "You need to be careful with eggs that—"

He suddenly noticed something through the window behind her.

Chickens.

Several of them were walking around a small grassy yard behind the clinic.

"Are those your chickens?" Bob interrupted.

Doctor Jess turned towards the window.

"They are."

"But you're a doctor. You must earn plenty of eggs."

Doctor Jess smiled.

"Doctors eat eggs too, Bob."

"And who knows," she continued. "Maybe one day I'll stop working here."

She glanced towards the chickens.

"And it would be nice to know I'll still have fresh eggs every morning."

CHAPTER 21

DINNER

Many years passed.

Bob kept buying healthy chickens whenever he had enough eggs to spare. His small flock grew into dozens of chickens. Then hundreds.

Eventually, he owned one of the largest chicken farms in Eggsville.

Every morning, his chickens laid more eggs than his old basket could ever have carried.

One evening, Bob invited his friends and neighbours to dinner at the farm.

Old Henry came too.

Everyone gathered around a long table while Bob brought out baskets filled with fresh eggs, bread and vegetables.

Henry looked outside towards Bob's enormous flock of chickens.

"What about that fat one over there?" he asked. "Should we cook her for the feast?"

Bob looked at the large chicken as he considered Henry's idea.

He knew she would certainly make for a good meal.

But he also knew that tomorrow she would lay a fresh egg.

And the day after that, another.

“I think we should leave the chicken alone,” he said. “She'll keep laying eggs, and we'll keep eating them.”

Henry reached for another egg.

“Eggs it is.”

That evening, everyone ate well.

Eat the eggs.

Grow the flock.

But never eat your chickens.

The story ends here.

The next chapter explains what Bob's chickens really mean.

FROM EGGS TO CASH

Eggsville is a made-up place, but almost everything that happens to Bob happens in real life.

The eggs are money.

Bob's factory represents a job. The basket shop represents a better job with more opportunities. Studying helps him develop new skills, while his pink baskets represent a small business—another way to earn extra money.

The eBasket represents the expensive things we sometimes want because they are new, fashionable or make us feel successful.

And then there are the chickens.

Healthy chickens represent investments that produce income. This could be shares in companies that pay dividends, a property that earns rent, or other investments that regularly produce money.

The eggs those chickens lay are the income produced by those investments.

Roosters represent growth investments. They don't produce eggs today, but they may become more valuable in the future.

Bob eventually discovers that earning money is only the beginning.

He can spend it.

He can save it.

Or he can use some of it to buy things that produce even more money.

That's the simple idea behind Bob's chickens.

Earn. Invest. Reinvest.

BUILDING YOUR FIRST FLOCK

So what does it actually mean to buy a healthy chicken?

For me, it means buying shares in good companies that regularly pay dividends.

When you buy shares, you own a small part of a company. If that company makes money, it may choose to return some of it to its shareholders.

That payment is called a dividend.

In Eggsville language, it's an egg.

LOOK FOR HEALTHY CHICKENS

Not every company that pays a dividend is a healthy chicken.

I like established businesses that have been paying reliable dividends for many years. I usually look back at least ten years—and twenty years is even better.

I also like companies that have grown their dividends over time. A reliable dividend is good. A reliable dividend that keeps growing is even better.

You can often see this clearly on a simple dividend-history graph.

EXAMPLE OF A HEALTHY DIVIDEND HISTORY

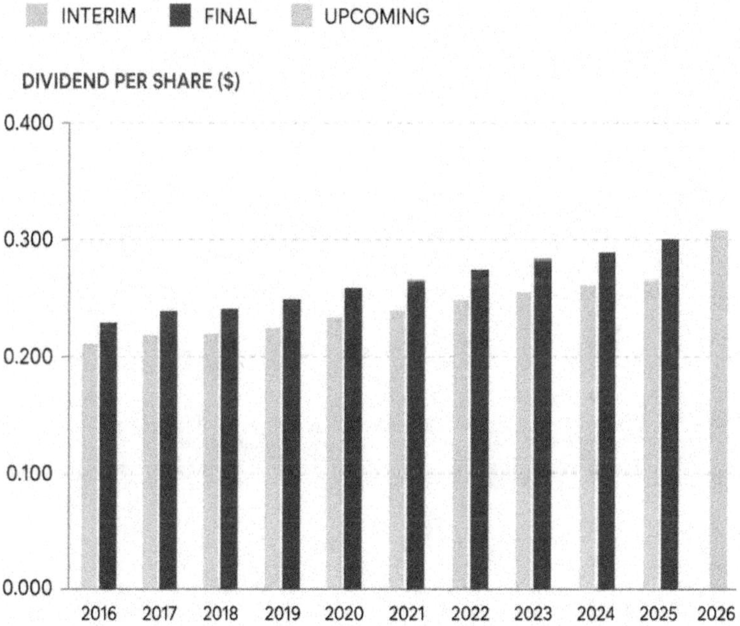

An example of what a healthy dividend history can look like.

This company pays two dividends each year—
an interim dividend and a final dividend.

Past dividends do not guarantee future payments.

When I look at a company, I ask a few simple questions:

- Has it paid reliable dividends for many years?
- Have those dividends generally grown over time?
- Is the business profitable and producing plenty of cash?
- Has it continued paying dividends through good years and difficult ones?

A company can offer a very large dividend today and still be a poor investment if it cannot keep paying it.

HOW MANY EGGS?

Dividend yield tells you how many eggs you receive for the money you invested.

If you invest $100 and receive $5 in dividends over a year, the dividend yield is 5%.

I personally tend to start by looking for companies with dividend yields of around 4–7%.

A much higher yield can look tempting, but sometimes it's high because the company is struggling and its dividend may not last.

This is called a dividend trap.

In Eggsville, it's the bargain chicken: plenty of eggs promised, but a chicken you may not be able to count on.

A cheap chicken is not a bargain if you cannot count on her eggs.

DON'T BUY JUST ONE CHICKEN

Even the healthiest chicken can get sick one day and stop laying.

Companies can have problems too, and dividends can be reduced or stopped.

That's why a dividend portfolio should contain good companies from different industries.

This is called diversification.

Think of your portfolio as your flock. If one chicken stops laying, the others can keep producing eggs.

LET THE EGGS BUY MORE CHICKENS

This is where dividend investing becomes really interesting.

Imagine your shares pay you $500 in dividends.

You could spend the $500.

Or you could use it to buy more shares, which may then produce dividends of their own.

You already know this system.

More chickens bring more eggs. More eggs bring more chickens.

Many companies offer a Dividend Reinvestment Plan, usually called a DRP. Instead of receiving your dividend as cash, it is used to acquire more shares in the company.

You can also receive the dividends as cash and choose which chickens to buy next.

Either way, the idea is the same:

Don't eat all the eggs while you are building the flock. Use them to buy more chickens.

WATCH THE FLOCK GROW

Reinvest your dividends and give your flock enough time, and something powerful can happen.

More shares produce more dividends, which can buy even more shares.

THE POWER OF DIVIDENDS REINVESTED

Starting with $10,000 and reinvesting all dividends.
Assumed dividend yield 5% and dividend growth 5% per year.

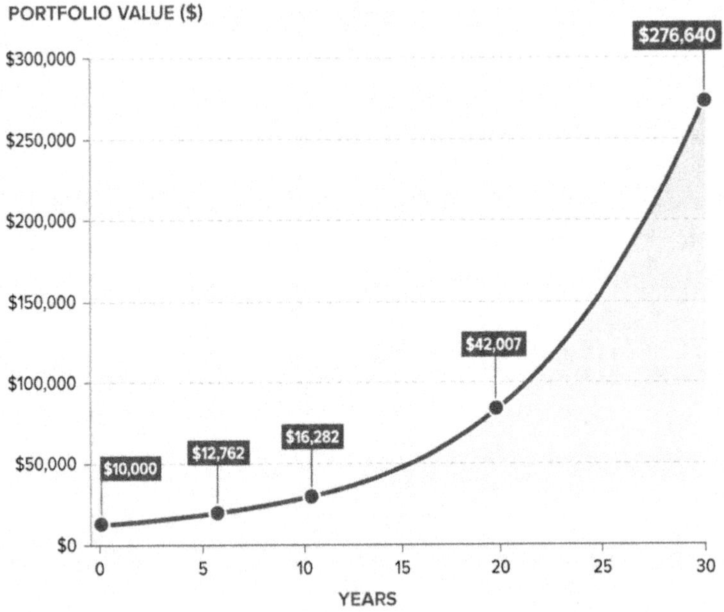

YEAR	0	5	10	15	20	25	30
PORTFOLIO VALUE	$10,000	$12,762	$16,282	$26,163	$42,007	$67,584	$276,640

For illustrative purposes only. Assumes annual dividend yield of 5% (paid and reinvested) and dividend growth of 5% per year. Does not take into account changes in share price, fees, taxes or inflation. Past performance is not a guarantee of future results.

KEEP AN EYE ON YOUR CHICKENS

Buying a healthy chicken doesn't mean it will stay healthy forever.

Every so often, check that the company is still doing well and that its dividends remain reliable.

Don't worry about every little movement in the share price.

What matters most is whether your chicken is still healthy and laying eggs you can count on.

NEVER EAT YOUR CHICKENS

Your chickens are the investments that produce your eggs.

If you sell a healthy chicken, you may receive money today—but that chicken will no longer be there to lay eggs for you tomorrow.

If a healthy chicken is still laying eggs I can count on, I generally prefer to keep it.

The goal isn't to keep buying and selling chickens.

It's to build a healthy flock, collect the eggs and let some of those eggs make the flock bigger.

ACKNOWLEDGMENTS

To my wife and children, thank you for listening to this story grow, sharing your ideas and helping bring Eggsville to life.

And to my mum, who always pushed me to keep learning and use that coconut-shaped thing on my shoulders.

ABOUT THE AUTHOR

Omer is an entrepreneur, investor and surfer. Most of his ideas have one thing in common: how to work less and surf more.

He wrote Never Eat Your Chickens to share the simple money lessons he wishes he knew when he was younger: earn, invest, reinvest—and give your chickens plenty of time to do their work.

Omer lives on the Northern Beaches of Sydney with his family. When he isn't working on another crazy idea, he enjoys travelling the world in search of warm water and good waves.

www.ingramcontent.com/pod-product-compliance
Lightning Source LLC
LaVergne TN
LVHW010738061126
851857LV00014B/1548
* 9 7 8 1 7 6 4 9 2 8 3 0 4 *